AF489205

MYSTERY
OF
MISERY

Henry al-Muthanna

Table of Contents

I. THE UPPER ROOM

V. $S = k \ln \Omega$

For
Henry Howard Chelune, Jack Vargas,
Terry McCrimmon, & Tony "Dutch" Ramos

Foreword

Have you ever wondered what it would be like to be inside
someone else's mind?
To know what they know, feel what they feel, see what they
see? To absorb the world as they do?

Henry al-Muthanna's *Mystery of Misery* offers a chance for
just that, a first person view of another's interpersonal rela-
tionship with themselves.

From delving into the depths of human emotionalism, to
sharp commentary on the harsh truths of navigating this
world as we know it.
These beautifully woven words truly give a first person view
of the intense and relatable journey of simply living in, re-
acting to, and processing the external complexities of exis-
tence.

Within these pages lives an honest hand to hold while you
make your way through those trenches. This book puts a
spotlight on the shrouded corners of this life that people
fear to face.

This book is a lesson... if you allow it to be.

- Cait Maree O'Shea

Preface

I never wanted to publish a book of poetry. It started
with the insistence of Tanay Sengupta, co-founder of
the Non-Aligned Poets Collective, who once remarked,
"The founder of NPC cannot host poetry conclaves
and book launches without having his own book."

Mystery of Misery has been three years in the making,
full of passion, love, and annoyance. For a while, I
thought it would never see the light of day, akin to the
decade-long wait for Guns N' Roses' Chinese Democ-
racy album. And yet, here it is: Henry al-Muthanna at
his most raw and honest, with *Mystery of Misery*.

Though the compilation, editing, and formatting of
Mystery of Misery has taken three years, this book has
been building inside me for forty-one years. It is sin-
gle-handedly the largest undertaking of my poetry
"career" (is poetry a career or a lifestyle? The jury
is still out on that). I toyed with the idea of not pub-
lishing for a plethora of reasons, the largest one being
imposter syndrome. As I muse in "Boom Bap": "Who
wants to listen to a white man gripe about his addic-
tions, afflictions, and all those forgotten reasons?"

Why the title?
Islam plays a large role in my life. The religion has
taught me to accept that all the good and the bad in
this world come from Allah for a greater reason or

lesson. Most times, however, I tend not to see any benefit in suffering. It is in this lack of vision for the grand plan that the title of this book was born.

The task is to accept the fact that I may never learn the reason for suffering, while utilizing this knowledge in everyday life, especially in more trying times, to grant myself some semblance of peace. Still, I am certain my rattled corporeal mind will always question the mystery of misery.

Mystery of Misery has been fragmented into five sections, each focusing on a particular aspect of life. Below is a breakdown of each section.

Section I, *The Upperroom*, is the most personal part of the book and was the hardest to write. Frankly, I was apprehensive about including some poems in this section, particularly "Paradise at the Feet," "PITIU," and "Patriarchal Disservice."

Section II, *Pilliful*, briefly looks at my struggle with prescription pills. It truly was the most disgusting part of my life.

Section III, *Al-Hind*, covers my six years living in India. My relationship with India can be described as a love-hate relationship. This section also contains my most popular poem in India, "Saar."

Section IV, *Sociopatas Sucios*, is Spanish for *Dirty Sociopaths*. It is here that I opine on the things wrong with society at large.

Rounding out *Mystery of Misery* is Section V, titled

$S = k \, ln \, \Omega$. The title is borrowed from the Boltzmann-Planck equation for entropy. This section is filled with esoteric lyrics and metaphysical poems.

Enjoy, and contemplate the *Mystery of Misery*.

Thank you for supporting independent poetry.

Stay Non-Aligned,

Henry al-Muthanna

MYSTERY
OF
MISERY

I

THE UPPER ROOM

Poet's Prayer

Oh Poetry,

I seek refuge from hubris and narcissism.

In the name of Poetry, most gaslight, most machinate.

Say: I will not recite what you recite
nor will you recite what I recite.

And I will not recite that
which you have been wont to recite
nor will you recite that
which I have been wont to recite.

To you be your poetry and to me mine.

Misty Roaming

In depths of grief and hopelessness,
I tread.
Burning bridges
a path misled.
Strong of heart
yet spirit weak and worn.
No more to please
nothing more to seek.
Past shackles shed, I explore
discovering a woman with shades
my soul's core.

Colors adorned my skin manifold,
pain and shame endured,
I try to break the bond
in dark moments
but faith is etched in stone
forever fond.
Unable to erase
nor cast away.
Love's testament remains.
Come what(ever) may.

Boom Bap

Expressing my emotions feels so strange.
Who wants to listen to a white man gripe about his
addictions, afflictions
and all those forgotten reasons?

A specter on the spectrum
whose equilibrium is severed.
If I had to gauge I would say
most of my rational thoughts have flown away.

I am not insane
more like asinine
the glass is half full
is it even mine?
Living off borrowed time
the glass half empty is clearly mine
come see in me
the culmination of decline.

Absolute absurdity is my blind self-hate.

Write it down!
Elaborate!

Poetry permits self-healing.
Is it too late?

Paradise at The Feet

My mother!
My mother!
Why do I write this if I cannot be bothered?

Grateful for the favor of giving me life
yet does one painful act
excuse four decades of mental solitude & strife?
What was there to gain by shunning me?
In your dying days, you say that you loved me?

You bore me,
then got bored of me
should have just aborted me
but you couldn't afford it, I see.

Never did I suckle your breast.
Day in,
day out
you shut me out.
Conceived,
then perceived
your lawful firstborn
son as an illegitimate seed
all because he was me.

Your insolent insistence instigated iniquities,
outside of love,
inside the grime

of vestibules,
trains,
parks in the rain.

Swore with all my might
that I would make it right.
Now there is Zahra,
embodiment of all you never were.
Luminosity such
it scatters your ashes afar.
Familial plight ended the night
I swore
kun faya kun
declaring my might.

(W)rites of the Father

You spit in your father's face?
Such a disgrace!
How can one disparage an unconditional embrace?
The root of it all,
you have trampled underfoot
with your arduous march!

Last has become first,
he too shall pass.

I grew up to understand,
that you inherited a rotten life.
For the salt of the earth,
all transgressions are in the past.

Bint

I love Zahra unconditionally.
That should be self-evident,
if you can't see.
I would kill for this child,
I know that sounds wild.
Though it is harder,
I try to live for this child.

It is amazing how I never wanted kids,
always looked at them in my mind as prison bids.
Zero to eighteen is far long.
It was fate, however, that showed me I was wrong.
Without my daughter,
I would surely falter.

She is the light of my eyes,
the peace of my heart,
the wisdom in my mind,
so I do not fault,
myself or others,
let alone she,
for Z is of me.

I have waited my whole life to meet you,
how on earth could I ever mistreat you?[1]

---

1. "Bint" is Arabic for "daughter of"

Calm Night

You are not what I wanted
you are what I needed.
You helped me move on inside
when I felt defeated.
Having helped to heal this mind
it is as if you mended a fractured part of time.
The cut was deep yet you cauterized and stitched the
wound.

Nestled in my heart,
you have built your own place.
I celebrate your grace through my art.
You are not my sunshine
but my Calm Night.

Duolingo

¡La traición es estúpida!
¡Silencio!
Mi tío está en llamas!
¡No hables!
Mi paciencia es nula.
¡Tu alma es mala!
¡Bailaré en tu tumba![1]

---

1. Translation:

Your betrayal was stupid!
Silence!
My uncle in flames!
Do not speak!
My patience is gone.
Your soul is evil!
I dance on your grave!

PITIU

Pity me.

For learned masters breached me,
preying on naiveté.
In fetus I lay,
while praying, no begging,
for this mental hurt to go away.

Divinely appointed leaders
delegate disorder and dismay.

I was to be the gold standard.
Alas abandoned,
left astray.

Where was thine mother?
Herself, smothered
with strife in lieu of love and life.

Pity me.
For learned masters breached me.

Impossible to reach me.

Hidden resentment,
under a reflective guise.

Do I choose…?

Son of an illiterate has become a poet,
so I know there is hope yet.
Shall it be spurned away?
Am I destined to be a failure?
Paternal gray?

My mind is frayed.

Focus.
You are not done yet.

I am nervous.
My palms are wet.

Pity me.
For learned masters breached me.

Fast Times at Ridgewood High

Worriedly wondering in street light,
the glare burns my eyes.
Empty stomach,
tired mind.
Is child abandonment not a crime?
Exception
not the rule
in this Greenish-White World.
Rush to my race?
Their economics manufactured my fate!

Where is my community?
One hand washes the other,
both wash the face!
Come together!
Make haste!

Support you?
We shall when the sky has two moons!

I know now unity is lunacy.

When I look up,
I perceive in UV God frowning at me.

Personal Judas

Heavy is the head
adorned with the cardboard crown.
For I am my Judas,
betrayal will always circle back around.

Humans of Islam

You bite your tongue at Allah?
Because I am human.

Yet, you still worship the Creator?
Because I am human.

Sure, but you dabble in haram[1].
Because I am human.

You sound a little lost.
Because I am human.

Is that two tabs on your tongue?
Because I am human.

____

1. Arabic for the word "forbidden." Typically used in Islamic Law.

Diluted Absolution

We stood shoulder to shoulder.
Truth of the matter is
you were a
fair-weather friend,
glorified associate.
Now it ends…

A house divided cannot stand
fed ill-wishes,
bad advice,
evil eye.

A result of dissolved composure and respect.

Brackish water,
a diluted dream.

My contemporary in contempt,
it is time to come clean.

As the gray smoke dissipates inside my lungs,
I see the truth rising like steam.

Personal peace prevails;
Ave! for the mutual animosity in our hearts.

I Need a New Pair of Specs

Second solar score approaching the fore!

Reflect in the smoke;
remember in the sky.

Discarded miserable hazards are recommended
against preserving a lie.

SHOW ME WHO I AM WITHOUT SSRIs!!!

Agitation,
delusions of calamity,
attained.

Frustration,
delusions of grandeur,
sustained.

Splendor,
I shall feign.

A faux fox in a foggy forest,
lingering
in that ubiquitous lull before the kill.

Genetic inhibitor inhibits
encompassing empathy effectively.
Medically it is called psychopathy.

If the feeling were a monarch,
I would be at court daily,
to bend mine knee for my Queen.
I have to listen
for what she denies me
sets me free.
Why revolt
under the guise of a pittance of hope?

Here we regret.
Here we lament.
Curses to thee who still dares to dream!

Yeah Man

My brother,
Word is you left to kick it with your mother.
If this is the case,
I need one last favor:
Go see my father;
let him know I'm good as can be.
Even without the ones I love,
I continue to breathe…

Mi gente,[1]
Mi hermano,[2]
Titles all earned.

The silver lining is you aren't stuffed in an urn.
Tu sabes[3], this year has been a disaster.
Muy malo [4]
How will I handle?

Mi primo[5],
Mi tio[6],
Titles all earned.

---

1. My people
2. My brother
3. You know
4. Very bad
5. My cousin
6. My uncle

Group Therapy

This isolation is getting to me.

Inmates are not rehabed whilist
serving in penitentiaries.

This I infer as I circumnavigate infinites.

Truly cannot comprehend what is happening to I
Self-bias subconscious emoter emoting a lie,
a ready made mask
to malign what's inside.
Mixed emotions
are getting to me.
Might be time for group therapy.
A session for the pain,
to wash it all away.
Want to purify,
need to be clean,
but that can never happen
for I am *miskeen*[1].
Just keep the faith,
smile in their face.
Somewhere along the way,
I lost my grace.

---

1. Arabic for "poor, miserable, or begger" in this poem the
context is miserable

Strangely YOLO

At times I feel as if a stranger in my own home.
This feeling is stronger than the Zionists Iron Dome.
Was that racist?
Nowadays, you cannot say,
what you need to say,
as we are surrounded by Snowflakes & Nazis,
and neither one can see.
No one wants honesty
they all just want lies from me.
Why can't they see
all I ever wanted to be
was just me?

Yet
I've always felt stuck,
caught in a perpetual rut.
No broken wings, just broken dreams,
having wings means to be angelic,
my situation is rather more hectic.

As these days pass,
I continue to get older,
soon I glean
this'll all be over.
Knowing my karma,
I'll start over,
reincarnated to a life form lower.
This because I will never get back what I put in.
In anyone's book, that isn't a win.

Big emotions strain my heart.
Prozac numbs my brain.
Told to go solo.
You only live once,
YOLO!

Who do I kid?
I'll never get back what I put in.

Patriarchal Disservice

I am a man.
Yet, how do I show it?
All I see is failure
but you wouldn't notice.
I eat these pills,
to dull the moment.
Do not want to cry,
that's not a man…
In all honestly,
I do not have a plan.
I need to feel love.
I want to bask in warm sun rays,
yet I am trapped in this mist,
a peasantry grey.

When trying to break the cycle,
we never realize it is us who must break.

The generational curse is in my DNA,
which gave a me a heavy heart,
a sad soul,
and all I simply needed
was to share in your world.

I tend to always be drifting,
stuck in a perpetual moment
where nothing seems uplifting.
Lost in the shuffle,
an everyday haze.

THIS lethargy,
THIS emotional army,
is out to conquer me,
but this is not me.

I am blinded through these drug-shot eyes.
To whom am I doing a disservice?

Yourself

Do I deserve this?

Karma comes around three times harder,
who knew drawing a breath would be so much drama?

*The cure to your aliment is within you and you do not know; and
your pain is also from you but you do not see.*[1]

---

1 Taken from a sermon of Imam Ali ibn Abi Talib found in *Peak of
Eloquence*

Toxic Mansplaining (Loud & Obnoxious)

Holding back tears,
it must be done.
Toxic masculinity,
perchance, I have some.

For a man to keep his emotion
exiled far away,
means an early grave.
A blind man's vision can be a grand
projection of manifested growth,
a spiritual mission.

Outward hate is a deflection
for subconscious personal rejection.
Tired of the self-affection and self-attention,
this desire for external love is a festering
human synaptic infection.

Abandonment issues,
is the reason for the tissues.

Yet, with you, trauma subsides!
Help me live!
I do not want to die,
eighty-percent ratio in men is far too high.

Sought to give back
from what had long been denied.
Took quite a while,
but I have finally awakened,

to the fact that
many intersections,
do not have to be hard life lessons.

Shock to the system,
then comes equilibrium.
Stands up to strife,
defying the nervous system,
simply by declaring:

I have direction!

Fermentation Without Representation

Anger,
a fermented drink.
It has been encased under pressure for so long,
with no room to think.
The slightest wrangling
pops the top off.
What goes up,
must come down.
Pressure was alleviated,
but for how long?

How many barrels of fermented drink
do I have to smash?
Or should I walk away & forget about the stash?

It goes down smooth, but then comes that kick...
Oh man!
The bitterness of this drink!

Anger,
I will not pour another glass,
Nor
will I pay my tab.

What have you done for me,
aside from plotting my end?
What gifts have you given?
What new thoughts laid bare?
This relationship is over.
I want fresh air.

Anger is slyly marketed as:

Emancipating

Intoxicating

Strengthening

Vindicating

When in reality…

it is imprisoning

II

PILLIFUL

Pharma Bro

Why sue Big Pharma?
I knew going in,
everyday life was crushing me,
from within.
What started as a physical ailment;
mental pain,
has spun out of control,
I have become recreationally sane.

As I pour these pills
out of the bottles,
listen as they crash like rain.
Impulse tells me
It'll ease our pain.
There is a fleeting notion in my brain
that they want us defeated,
medicated prey.

When I am sober
I come back to my mind.
Between the highs
I acknowledge
I am destroying my liver
I don't have much time.
I shake
I quiver
afraid I will be a zombified sleepwalker
who drives into the river.

Gag Reflex

It happened yet again,
gagged mid-swallow.
This choking reflex
resurrects inner thoughts.

Reflecting on regret.
I fell into familial failure,
took thirty-eight years
for me to become
a walking contradiction.

Mental notifications went off;
muscle tension followed,
reminded yet again
how this will end
losing family & all of my friends.
This is just the beginning of all things to end.
The end of all things to come
is when I am wrapped in a kafan[1].
Life is done.

Do I want my daughter to know I died
a junkie on a cold, random floor?

For us the pillifull,
it's abominable

------

1   A kafan is a Muslim burial shroud

for the pitifully profitable
it is phenomenal.
It is on Pfizer to turn off the gushing pill geyser.

For how long can one wax poetic
about a troubled tryst with tablets
on their tablet?

Until then
I search for self-control
in an increasingly apathetic world.

What Would You Do For A Klondike Bar?

Please do not try what I yearn in my heart for,
not for the love of a woman,
but a vice even worse that will ruin.
For tis' the drugs I adore.
Taste of divinity on my tongue,
succulent sweet embrace coming through my pores.
Embraced
I am raised degrees above the masses.
Such euphoria suggests
forsake that rhyme scheme passion…

Give it to me,
let me fall as
pupils morph into pills
with eyes wide shut.
Whilst sitting in a position of Lithium Lotus,
seeking to medicate & recreate.

Prostrating in the pharmaceutical prayer space,
to the one draped in pure,
white medical robes
wearing a rosary stethoscope.
I am one with the priestly pharmacist.
Zoloft communion.
Flesh of my flesh
I offer in sacrifice
this my liver.

As I swirl in my mouth ritually pure LSD,
I begin to think,
what is wrong with me?
In trying to break the matrix,
I ruined me!

Fluctuations of Fluoxetine

Depression can be heaven
because I let no one in.
Do not want be lonely,
just leave me alone.

Even in my home,
as ungrateful drug-addled drone.
I mope and I moan.

ONCE AGAIN CAN YOU JUST LEAVE ME ALONE!?

Ostracized & exiled,
I'll be here for a while.
Only thing that helps
is getting smacked by Zac
He is a pro,
who motivates me to go.

Como Blanco/Hazme Toto

What am I doing up?
An insomniac,
that's fucked up.
Ambien gets me high,
Ambien gets me by,
That is
until I am on the floor foaming at the mouth.

Why can't I help me?
Why did I shut me out?

Depression is real.
Lack of purpose is real.
I do not want to live just to deal,
I want to live for something real.

Why can't I help me?

Why can't I help?

Why can't I?

Why can't?

Why?

?

III

AL-HIND

Guest Rights

Not a guest anymore,
yet not one of you.
So I lost my privileged god status.
What am I to do aside from patiently persevere?

There is an exceptionalism in the air,
although not the scent of jasmine.
All I perceive is the stench of fires abounding,
smog encircles this already clouded mind.

This blanket of smoke is making me sick!

What happened to dharma?
Is the state of the nation a result of Bharat's karma?

There are questions continuously asked
inside my mind:

Can I be myself,
though this is not my land?
Should I now ignore sensitivities,
Cultural and religious?

For what this society ignores under an air of feigned
ignorance is truly just malicious.

Head Trip Drama

Swirling my head are all the things they said:

Take back your agency.

You have too much trauma.
You are less than human.

Man, you really took a bullet for me.
Knowing now how they act, I could never work with them.

Why should we take orders from a white foreigner?

In the end, it is yours.
We support you no matter what.

You are scum.

When people see it, they think of you.

I can't believe this I need my space.

No, this is not in your head.
It happened.

He has a god complex.

Some people do not like to take orders.

You don't owe them anything.

This was the shot in the arm the city needed.

I am more personable than you!
Go find a park and sit on a bench.

I was surprised at the announcement.
You barely know them.

You didn't push me out.
I forgive you.

I was upset you didn't come to me.
When I heard the news, I said to myself, "it will collapse."
I knew this but felt you weren't ready to hear it.

In my interactions with them the word "disingenuous"
comes to mind.

I am surprised it happened so fast, in only two months.

Who runs it,
us or him?

Noodle Dick

Rushing while she's loitering,
noodle dick.
Scruffy-looking thirst trap,
noodle dick.
Ungrateful,
lacking introspection,
noodle dick.
No inner monologue,
noodle dick.
Focus on your level up,
noodle dick.
Less shame than a mic organizer,
noodle dick.
Balls dropped
doesn't make a man now,
noodle dick.
One choice away from groping on the train,
ya noodle dick.
Always coming late but never ever cums,
that noodle dick.
No respect,
not even for your mother,
noodle dick.
Learned it from your father,
all your misogyny,
noodle dick.

Day In the Life

Pooja bells,
muezzin yells.

Aunties stare;
I don't care.

Burning fumes,
children with no shoes.

Bribes collected,
institutions detested.

Auto scam
cancels plans.

Salaam Meets Namaste

Namaste,
nah, I mean stay.
I see the light in you.
Why do you seek to snuff out
what the world likes in you?

True love jihad is the struggle to love oneself.

Come,
I'll break my fast,
so we can break bread.

We are all we got.

Come, Ahki,
eat from my pot,
drink from my jug,
meditate on my prayer rug.

Like I said, bhaiya,
we are all we got.

Salaam meets Namaste,
a righteous pair!
We are separate but equal;
that is spiritually fair.

Ma-lè[1]

Nestled in my chair,
I hear you falling to the ground
rush to my balcony
in a three-sixty, I turn,
you are everywhere.

Ma-lé falling on me,
allows me to dream
that the sins of this city
ma-lé will wash away clean

---

1 Ma-lè is Kannada for rain.

Saar

Saar,
Myself like all things that you give.
With my hand out,
Saar,
please give.

Myself no make a lot of rupees, Saar.
Help me,
Saar.

Myself need:
Kg of rice,
Kg of flour.

Saar,
yourself go to the Moon.
Myself want to live.

IV

SOCIÓPATAS SUCIOS

Unipolar Unity

The tribe is scattered!
We have no community!
Enough of this posturing over unipolar unity!
You invert the symbols,
flip the hate.
You claim to bring peace,
yet only desecrate.

This is your life's purpose?
Wake up from that devilish dream!

We do not wish to be accepted,
we will not acquiesce.

*Join the hive mind,
you have nothing left.*

We will never cede our autonomy:
We can never just assimilate.
It is fate that guides us to a special place?
Destiny declares that we drink from this poetic lake.

New Millennium Tribal War

Red or blue,
saffron or green,
colors contrived to exaggerate your fears.
To blindly hate your neighbor is an
unforgivable communal sin.

We the People
get tribal over sports teams.
Elites, knowing this,
try to divide.
Tribal over trivial,
is the sign of the times!

We the People
do not talk to each other.
We the People
often look past each other.
There is no reason why
I could not call you
sister or brother,
as we come from the same Source Code.

Blue-collar united is the fear of the Elites!
Blue-collar united, peacefully, in the streets!
A commonality runs through us all.
Together we pull on their string of lies,
watch it unfurl!

Socioeconomic
the true color is green.
Red
white
or brown,
north
or south,
what does that mean?

New millennium tribal warfare
I do not want to kill my neighbor.

ATL Alone

The dome is gold;
so are the streets.
They've been deprived of their humanity,
so they piss at your feet.
People are hungry;
they have nothing to eat.
Thoughts and prayers
is a low-carb diet.
Yet you wonder
why the plebeians riot?

Ebenezer Church
has become Ebenezer Scrooge.
They just want the tithe;
they don't care about you,
Black Lives Matter,
or human rights.
Dr. King is dead,
we lost the fight.

Imagine Zombies

Imagine,
the Secularists' hymn.
With lyrics so beautiful is how they cope,
although the meaning
does not leave their throats.

Culturally Lennon, and
politically Lenin.
A broken value system,
akin to a deflowered virgin's hymen.

Zombified masses,
cranberry-colored glasses.

Post hoc fallacies
your train of thought is illogical;
the core of the concept is hollow.
Swallow the truth,
inside you are shallow.
To you ideological swallows,
I will not follow.

Free Range

Our chicken is free range,
yet our children are in cages,

Somewhere along the way,
society regressed
rather than progressed.
Colorful hair
meant you had a spine
now it signifies
all you do is whine.

What about me?
What about Raven?

Take that defeatist mindset to your safe haven.
Let him keep his boyhood,
he is only nine.
Gender swapping kids
should be a crime.

Any dissenting view,
you label them a racist,
or a bitter old man
not up on the times.

Meta

Welcome to the Meta-Verse.
What is Reality?
You do the guesswork.
I am tired of the pussyfooting.
Who is next for a premeditated cyber-death?
Let the algorithm pick next.
Are we the dead and departed actually alive?
What happens after the power cuts?
Stay on the broadband line,
ask ChatGPT,
Though it's answer is a guess at best!

The algorithm knows how to manipulate
your brainwave patterns to make you scared.
Continue to over share
who do you feel safer with
man or bear?
Generalized and compartmentalized
is your hate.

Doom scrolling through armageddon
with a blue light glare in your eye.
Where is the eye of the tiger?
Has your motivation completely died?
How can I be content?
Is it by making content that no one views?
I see you in my stories watching from afar.
Whether here or in the Meta-Verse,
you will never know who you are.

Dead Internet Theory

Godless consumer life.
Smart home pollution.
Distracted masses
is the modern solution!
Digital textiles,
wrist & eyes.
Starlink is now embedded in your mind.
Technological singularity is advertised as faux divinity.
While agentic AI runs amok behind the screen.

So goodbye to the lie,
that we all independent minds.
I will make the world as I see fit!,
this main character arrogance is humanity's decline.

We are all self-absorbed,
social media whores.
Who are we kidding?
We have blood on our keyboards.
Trading lives for likes.
Screens don't flatter.
Who will be the first
to post their suicidal splatter?

For every soul must taste death,
an event decreed.
In worrying about you,
I forgot about me!

Me First & The Gimmie Gimmies

Do not want to listen,
only wish to be heard.
I want to be followed,
does that sound absurd?
Haven't figured it out yet?
It is all about me.
View the IG Live;
stream a couple of tracks.
Reciprocity?
Please!
Your content is trash!
I will not provide feedback,
I'll leave you in the lurch.
At the open mic,
I am like a pastor in church.
I finally have authority.
What I say is fact.
The truth is in my feelings.
How do you not believe that?
I never graduated high school,
I have no degrees, so
I have to make this IG creative life all about me.
Monetize my life,
it's every aspect.
I expect the world,
but will give nothing back.

Content Creator/Constant Hater

Everyone is a Content Creator.
Everyone is a constant hater.

Vainglorious.
Shallow.

Humans?
Greater than animals?
We are easily the dumbest of mammals.
Vicegerent of Earth,
Yet we destroy the world around us.

Most sit idly by,
passing their time before they die.
It will be their grandchildren who ask:

Why…?

Rearrange

People grow apart,
drift away.
Hit the baseline,
it's time to rearrange.
Have they actually changed,
or has social media rotted their brain?

Post what you want,
post what you feel.
However my intuition is
you post it for mass appeal.
No one is trying to kill you.
You are actually quite safe.
All of this around us is manufactured hate.

Goat of Saturn

Your contentment created this resentment.
Numbers and stars?
It is time to pull your card.
Although it isn't a tarot,
you are as warped as a rabid animal.

Triple eight
Quadruple one

Numerology is real!
The Goat of Saturn tells me.

Manifest goodness,
kiss the sky.
It is time you got poked in your Third Eye.

Every lie has a little bit of truth.
The calm before the storm
is the witch reading your palm.
This black magic tempest
will be your downfall.

Strive To Survive

There once was a girl who was smart & sharp.
Dropout kings saw her only as thick & dark.
This dragon queen solved binomials,
quadratic equations,
destined for a Nobel nomination.

Innately in her hobby is where she found zen,
in bed
with her legs spread.

Ran with her libido and took the DL.
For no prize, however prestigious,
was worth giving into societal whims.

Katana sharp wit.
then she gave it up,
and slit her wrists.

Addicted to sex
she really couldn't flex
her brain anymore.
People in the neighborhood,
calling her a whore
but I knew better.
Didn't let her slip.
She grabbed my hand,
but couldn't get a grip.
Fell into the abyss
known as AIDS,
forever lost now in that maze.

She is a dear friend
I love her to death;
really do not want to see her take her last breath.
Medicine cocktails keeping her alive.
Now the game is: strive to survive.

New Normal

Social distancing,
new normal,
the world has never been so formal.

Disease and sickness reign in the air
Old and young die;
now that is fair.

Equal opportunity,
no faith can save,
no cure to avail.

Cover up and disinformation,
shame upon all the nations.
What started in China ends with you.

Fait Accompli

Getting online
claiming to Fight the Power!
Then why do you wait until the time of the hour?
Armchair activist here to save the day!
Who asked for your virtual help anyway?

Flag emoji
with a digital fist raised
we know you will visit Dubai anyway.

Party of God
where is your zeal?

You chant:

AL QUDS! AL QUDS!

What about Kabul?

Are we supposed to care?
Killing Shias is fait accompli.

You cannot be concerned
that a Twelver mother mourns.

Ideological
scorn sways your mind.

From the river to the sea,
we know the Shias
are your real enemy.

Ethically Cleansed

They were dirty
so we ethically cleansed.

We are the Lions of Judah
-in our own heads-

This is the fall of Jerusalem with Wi-Fi,
-it is has been said-

Trail of Tears in the modern era,
a Zionist's dream

Was the painter right?
Was the painter wrong?
In the end
his ends did not justify the means
I mean
his means did not justify the ends

This I think
as I lay dying
This I think
as you lay buying.

What I need to do is
to drag a joint
past the point
of no return
to ancestral lands.

Keep calm?
They are my clan!
mAsses tight lipped
imitating a clam.

Body harvesting
as the world needs spleens
How many little girls lost the gleam in their eyes
surprised by their desire to die?

Light up the fireworks
over a domed sky!
Light up the fireworks
over a doomed sky!
Bright like Independence Day
humanity has died.
We should all be tried
by a court of jeers
our jury will be the ghosts of young people
who will never be peers.

No Piers,
do you condemn?
I am having trouble
wrapping your position
around my head.

It's freedom for everybody or it's freedom for nobody!
as Malcolm said.

I assist in their resistance
my stance is clear.

Desire for life
burns brighter than any bush.
You are not the people of Musa
this is clear.

V

$$S = k \ln \Omega$$

Welcome Home

For too long,
you have forgotten who you are,
where you come from,
how far you have gone.

Fire snuffed out,
embers remain.
Time to fan the flame;
douse with self-confidence,
arrogance they'll claim.
Reroute to reclaim,
rise to remain.
The bleak shall be left on the earth;
the meek are slain.
Do not yearn for the leftovers of a tyrant's gain.

Coming back to clarity allows one to
project their pain.
Steadfast insecurities
are all that was gained.
As information cannot be destroyed,
lasting memories are disdained.

Roar of the Toddler

Choco milky, milky choco,
shared its udders strictly.
The birdies, the birdies,
are in relation to the axis and the hand-mill.
Flood wawa cannot reach.
Handed over the mirror,
to see the position.

You want pop!?
I don't want,
I want,
I don't want.
What do you say?
Please.

Think.
Hmmm…
Blinding light
is in the sky.
Are you there, little elephant?
I can see you,
you're looking at me!
Hide and seek,
car car is there?

In the absence, down came the choco milky, milky choco,
to wash the patience out.
Out came the wiser,
to dry up all of me,
to be akin to,
ABC is 1-2-3.

Higher ground
looks down.
Prickling in the eye,
suffocating chest,
only to be denied to drink from Mama's breast.
Intended not…
Mama, is it my fault?
Look, I do.
I did.
Clap hands, Chinnu, you did good.

Come,
I did choo choo,
made mess.
Let me see,
let me see.
New nappy?
Open your legs!
HAHAHA!

By surprise,
rushing forth,
neurotic synapses
tearing the seams,
so nap time now it seems.

World appeared glittering,
take new dress,
to be caressed in the cove.
Breakfast was at eight-thirty,
I was told.
Nappy wet again,
water play.

Leave the children there all day.

Gluttony of the oppressor,
Hunger of the oppressed
No better than the sneezing of a goat.

Partition Spacetime

Stare up to the Heavens as they crack open;
photons appear at all points upon creation
unwavering yet bent
by black hole eyes.
Extinction of light by absorption nebulae
such an experience for corporeals
is unfathomable in their minds.

Placate existence along narrow lines,
sentience to apes
was pearls to swine.

It is time to
partition spacetime.

As youth carry worms to the graves of their elders,
their offerings contrived,
lament laid bare
scorned at the alter of black widows.
The spiders have been kissed;
enchant the spell.

Placate existence along narrow lines,
sentience to apes
was pearls to swine.

It is time to
partition spacetime.

Lost like butterflies affected by alcoholism
lured by the promises of carnivorous hearts,
lulled by the melodies of irrational minds.

Placate existence along narrow lines,
sentience to apes
was pearls to swine.

It is time to
partition spacetime.

Rabbit Hole

Lethargically laying in bed
whilst numerical code runs down my eyes.

Inquisitively introspective

If this is Simulation,
then what happens to code upon deletion?

Symbiotic vibrational oneness
flows in minuscule ebbs
and Universe
why manifest your proofs
in such a flippant manner?

In perpetuity
trappings & sustenance were to be
bequeathed to all ungrateful children
of the Last Adam.

Collective dimensional shame.

The announcement is made

Synergistically the dissonance is far too great.
The command to withhold is incumbent. You must wait.

Situational awareness
time to find an exit
shall I open the Locust Door?

Subscription To Men's Health Monthly

I cry to you,
as he cried to me.
Genetic translucence cubes the line.

With tears in our eyes we view spatial realities
outside of time
allowing us to circle round in unity
until there are no sides.

This ringing bell does not offer salivation,
There is no salvation for the apes who are despised.
No desire for crises on infinite Earths,
when offered paradoxes as solutions.

Ignored is the spiritual drift,
dogma has created endemic riffs
Focused on a golden-grey horizon
no thoughts in the present tense,
poles flipped
result of mental seismic shifts

North Star in the Southern Sky.
Subject to the obstinate & shallow.
Self unaware.
Remove the traces of humanity;
even from the marrow!

I have outsourced, the job of caring.

Waste Not...

Not everything created is divine.
I am the essence of God!
How asinine!
The Eternal Ethereal
does not mingle with Creation
such a belief is a deep deviation.

What is heard in my head
was not whispered from above.
Light shining bright
caresses the sons of man,
who upon realizing that flagrancy
is the order of the day
have become mentally circumcised
with their hands tied.
Feigned spirituality in a blue-light-hell
leaves their vision drained.

Humanity has plateaued,
raising my ire
like a stubbed toe.

Hedonistically bewildered wandering
naked throughout the land.
Hyper-individualism this capitalist brain.

With such conduct I have self-exiled from my clan.

Trickle-Down Aggression

The flies have made their meals
above the rubbish bin.
With rubber in their heads
& calcified hearts
insincere incels become empathic eunuchs.
Fear is severed
with a clean cut,
desire incinerated to ash.
Spread across witch hazel,
the time has passed.

Gleaming
bright-eyed
like flame under a spoon.
Some chase dreams
others chase dragons.
All hamsters on a wheel,
your goal
is your pain.

Bemoaning screams echo from all sides.
Prometheus
looking down on the raging global fires,
remarks:

*I simply brought them a gift;
how should I have known?*

If a person is hurt in the forest,
do they make a sound?

Fusion Trunks

Ghee is hot,
sizzling on the tawa.
Who is siphoning away my energy at this hour?
Chicken is broiled
ecstasy soiled

Who will (I) foil my plans?
Thwarted by ancestral schemes.
Genetic blasts from the past,
fated by times chance.
Habitual circumcision,
I self inflict with this incision
to plant the seeds
I will be the flowers brought to me!

Test the gonads
the goal is clear
though I fear the ramifications of this test
in such an early year

Tawa cools aside an old man
sitting on the windowsill

Too many pills; too little time.
Wailing to the nurse is how I pass the time!

Cells divide,
trunks are clean.
Destroyed the whole Moon,
in a monkey's gleam.

Tawa washed.
Fresh and clean.

Who will be the distraction of I?
Suicide awareness is a game of I spy.
Time dies when you are bludgeoning fun.
Self aware now,
what have I done?

Test the gonads,
the goal is clear,
though, I fear the ramifications of this test
in such an early year

Searching For Satellite Signal

Frolic towards the Singularity,
wearing ribbons & bows.
Time in the tesseract,
how does that flow?

Existential dread,
aether reality of nothingness.
Clutching
at the pearls of String Theory
weak like gravity
which also permeates dimensions.

Straightened the Double Helix.
Connection to the Source Code,
severed.

By letting go
I have reformatted the soul.

Transmigrate Out of Parallels

Call them to their stations,
while you abandon yours.
Say a prayer for the porcelain baby lying on the floor.

Opened Pandora's box
to only find her heart
entrusted
with this translucent treasure
is how the paradox starts.
Lures me to a place
outside of time
takes me to a space
outside of my mind.
Now in this paradox
forever I am confined.

Master!
Oh, my Master!
Where are you now?
If You can do anything,
remove this furrow from my brow.

Why has He abandoned us,

His devotion to Spirituality,
superficial.

Their knowledge amassed,
artificial.

Her radiance illuminated,
feigned.

Time has now offered us
to journey back to start,
to transmigrate out of parallels
consisting of interconnecting circles.
Locking away the paradox,
permits us to go back,
will we make the same mistakes?
Is it all foretold?

Call them to their stations,
while you abandon yours.
Say a prayer for the porcelain baby lying on the floor.

Orange Tree

Pray, say to the Ganges
what do you see?
Light emanating from inside of you?
Inside of me?
On this solar plane of existence,
we expend cosmic radiation
as we ascend
the red shift burns faint.

Toiled countless epochal lives & cyclical deaths,
to finally take this rested breath.

We know for you the distance was great.
However, be patient, my child, you must wait.

Beyond the observable
is where we begin to guide the camel through
the eye of a needle for all to see!

Perceiving you in neon green,
voicing you in black.

Manifested mission,
chakras hidden.

Not of this time.
Forlorn care.

Shifted here by destiny,
Universe do what you want
for you are my mind.

Everything & Nothing

I am everything at once,
and yet nothing at all.
Conscious of this terrestrial plane's universal
uniqueness
allows me to bend to the will of Divine Oneness.

My God sets me free.

I booked passage on the ark of tranquility
sailing away questioning the mystery of misery.

With humility,
I absorb humiliation.

*Hate thyself
to know thyself,*
such a mindset, is mental suicide.

The note will simply read:
I tried…

Duality nuzzled at the center of serenity,
opacity.

Three dimensional life,
Two dimensional mind.
Vivisect all convergences.

My God sets me free.

I booked passage on the ark of tranquility,
sailing away questioning the mystery of misery.